MAD  LIBS®

KID LIBS MAD LIBS

I will not play Mad Libs during math.
I will not play Mad Libs during math.
I will not play Mad Libs during math.
I will not play Mad Libs during math.
I will not play Mad Libs during math.
I will not play Mad Libs during math.
I will not play Mad Libs during math.

By Roger Price and Leonard Stern

PSS!
PRICE STERN SLOAN

ISBN 0-8431-2827-5

2003 Printing

PSS! and *MAD LIBS* are registered trademarks of Penguin Putnam Inc.

MAD LIBS
INSTRUCTIONS

MAD LIBS® is a game for people who don't like games!
It can be played by one, two, three, four, or forty.

• RIDICULOUSLY SIMPLE DIRECTIONS

In this tablet you will find stories containing blank spaces where words are
left out. One player, the READER, selects one of these stories. The READER
does not tell anyone what the story is about. Instead, he/she asks the other
players, the WRITERS, to give him/her words. These words are used to fill
in the blank spaces in the story.

• TO PLAY

The READER asks each WRITER in turn to call out a word—an adjective or
a noun or whatever the space calls for—and uses them to fill in the blank
spaces in the story. The result is a MAD LIBS® game.

When the READER then reads the completed MAD LIBS® game to the other
players, they will discover that they have written a story that is fantastic,
screamingly funny, shocking, silly, crazy, or just plain dumb—depending
upon which words each WRITER called out.

• EXAMPLE (*Before* and *After*)

" _____ !" he said _____
        EXCLAMATION   ADVERB

as he jumped into his convertible _____ and
                     NOUN

drove off with his _____ wife.
            ADJECTIVE

" *Ouch!* !" he said *Stupidly*
        EXCLAMATION   ADVERB

as he jumped into his convertible *cat* and
                     NOUN

drove off with his *brave* wife.
            ADJECTIVE

In case you have forgotten what adjectives, adverbs, nouns, and verbs are, here is a quick review:

An ADJECTIVE describes something or somebody. *Lumpy, soft, ugly, messy,* and *short* are adjectives.

An ADVERB tells how something is done. It modifies a verb and usually ends in "ly." *Modestly, stupidly, greedily,* and *carefully* are adverbs.

A NOUN is the name of a person, place or thing. *Sidewalk, umbrella, bridle, bathtub,* and *nose* are nouns.

A VERB is an action word. *Run, pitch, jump,* and *swim* are verbs. Put the verbs in past tense if the directions say PAST TENSE. *Ran, pitched, jumped,* and *swam* are verbs in the past tense.

When we ask for a PLACE, we mean any sort of place: a country or city *(Spain, Cleveland)* or a room *(bathroom, kitchen.)*

An EXCLAMATION or SILLY WORD is any sort of funny sound, gasp, grunt, or outcry, like *Wow!, Ouch!, Whomp!, Ick!,* and *Gadzooks!*

When we ask for specific words, like a NUMBER, a COLOR, an ANIMAL, or a PART OF THE BODY, we mean a word that is one of those things, like *seven, blue, horse,* or *head*.

When we ask for a PLURAL, it means more than one. For example, *cat* pluralized is *cats*.

MAD LIBS® is fun to play with friends, but you can also play it by yourself! To begin with, DO NOT look at the story on the page below. Fill in the blanks on this page with the words called for. Then, using the words you have selected, fill in the blank spaces in the story.

Now you've created your own hilarious MAD LIBS® game!

RULES FOR RIDING ON THE SCHOOL BUS

ADJECTIVE _____

NOUN _____

VERB _____

ADJECTIVE _____

NOUN _____

PART OF THE BODY _____

ADJECTIVE _____

TYPE OF CONTAINER _____

PLURAL NOUN _____

VERB _____

NOUN _____

PLURAL NOUN _____

VERB ENDING IN "ING" _____

PLURAL NOUN _____

ADJECTIVE _____

ADVERB _____

ADJECTIVE _____

MAD LIBS®
RULES FOR RIDING
ON THE SCHOOL BUS

1. Every morning, your bus runs a/an _____ route, so you
   <u>ADJECTIVE</u>

   must be sure that you arrive at your local _____ early.
   <u>NOUN</u>

2. While waiting, do not _____ in the middle of
   <u>VERB</u>

   the street. You might get run over by a/an _____ _____.
   <u>ADJECTIVE</u>   <u>NOUN</u>

3. When you see the bus, wave your _____.
   <u>PART OF THE BODY</u>

4. Before boarding, make sure you have all of your _____ books
   <u>ADJECTIVE</u>

   and your lunch _____.
   <u>TYPE OF CONTAINER</u>

5. When you board the bus, do not push or jostle any of the smaller

   _____. Go to the nearest empty seat and _____.
   <u>PLURAL NOUN</u>   <u>VERB</u>

6. Do not talk to the _____ while the bus is in motion.
   <u>NOUN</u>

7. Do not throw _____ at the other students.
   <u>PLURAL NOUN</u>

8. Instead of wasting time by _____, use the trip to
   <u>VERB ENDING IN "ING"</u>

   study your _____.
   <u>PLURAL NOUN</u>

9. Follow these rules and you will have a/an _____ ride and
   <u>ADJECTIVE</u>

   arrive _____ at your _____ school.
   <u>ADVERB</u>   <u>ADJECTIVE</u>

From KID LIBS® • Copyright © 2001, 1990 by Price Stern Sloan,
a division of Penguin Putnam Books for Young Readers, New York.

MAD LIBS® is fun to play with friends, but you can also play it by yourself! To begin with, DO NOT look at the story on the page below. Fill in the blanks on this page with the words called for. Then, using the words you have selected, fill in the blank spaces in the story.

Now you've created your own hilarious MAD LIBS® game!

FIELD TRIP TO A FARM PART I

NOUN _____

CELEBRITY (FEMALE) _____

ADJECTIVE _____

VERB _____

TYPE OF FOOD _____

ANOTHER TYPE OF FOOD _____

TYPE OF LIQUID _____

ADJECTIVE _____

COLOR _____

NOUN _____

EXCLAMATION _____

SILLY WORD _____

PLURAL NOUN _____

COLOR _____

PLURAL NOUN _____

ANIMAL (PLURAL) _____

ADJECTIVE _____

ANIMAL NOISE _____

MAD LIBS®
FIELD TRIP TO A FARM PART I

Last week, our _____ teacher, Ms. _____ , took our
　　　　　　　　NOUN　　　　　　　　　　CELEBRITY (FEMALE)

whole _____ class on a field trip to a local farm so we could
　　　　　ADJECTIVE

see how farmers _____ . That morning, we packed our knap-
　　　　　　　　　　　VERB

sacks with _____ and _____ and filled our
　　　　　TYPE OF FOOD　　　　　ANOTHER TYPE OF FOOD

thermoses with _____ . Then we drove to the farm and
　　　　　　　　　TYPE OF LIQUID

met the farmer, who was a/an _____ man wearing _____
　　　　　　　　　　　　　　　　ADJECTIVE　　　　　　　　COLOR

overalls and a straw _____ on his head. He shook hands with
　　　　　　　　　　　　NOUN

me and said, "_____!" Then he showed us the big round
　　　　　　　　　EXCLAMATION

tower called a _____ where he stores his _____ .
　　　　　　　　SILLY WORD　　　　　　　　　　　　PLURAL NOUN

He also gave us a tour of his _____ barn that was full of hay
　　　　　　　　　　　　　　　　COLOR

and dried _____ . There were stalls in the barn for horses
　　　　　　　PLURAL NOUN

and _____ , so the place really smelled _____ .
　　　ANIMAL (PLURAL)　　　　　　　　　　　　　　　　ADJECTIVE

We met the farmer's wife who was in the backyard of the farm house

feeding chickens, that ran around saying, "_____."
　　　　　　　　　　　　　　　　　　　　　　　ANIMAL NOISE

MAD LIBS® is fun to play with friends, but you can also play it by yourself! To begin with, DO NOT look at the story on the page below. Fill in the blanks on this page with the words called for. Then, using the words you have selected, fill in the blank spaces in the story.

Now you've created your own hilarious MAD LIBS® game!

FIELD TRIP TO A FARM PART II

ADJECTIVE_____

ANIMAL NOISE _____

COLOR_____

ADJECTIVE_____

TYPE OF VEHICLE _____

ADJECTIVE_____

TYPE OF FOOD _____

ANIMAL _____

ADJECTIVE_____

ADJECTIVE_____

ADVERB_____

SOMETHING LARGE _____

ADJECTIVE_____

ANOTHER TYPE OF FOOD _____

ANOTHER TYPE OF FOOD _____

ADJECTIVE_____

PLURAL NOUN _____

VERB ENDING IN "ING" _____

TYPE OF LIQUID _____

MAD LIBS®
FIELD TRIP TO A FARM PART II

Many foods we eat came from some kind of _____ farm.
                                          ADJECTIVE

Farmers raise cows that say "_____" and give us fresh,
                            ANIMAL NOISE

_____ milk. Kids who drink lots of milk grow up _____.
COLOR   ADJECTIVE

Our teacher took us out to a field where we saw the farmer driving

his _____. He was plowing the _____ field so that
    TYPE OF VEHICLE   ADJECTIVE

he could plant _____. Nearby were his corn fields, where
               TYPE OF FOOD

the corn grew as high as a/an _____'s eye. The farmer grinds
                              ANIMAL

his corn and makes a/an _____ mash that he feeds to his pigs.
                        ADJECTIVE

Pigs, of course, are _____ animals that eat very _____
                     ADJECTIVE   ADVERB

and are shaped like _____. Pigs eat _____
                    SOMETHING LARGE   ADJECTIVE

food that consists mostly of _____ mixed with
                             ANOTHER TYPE OF FOOD

_____. These _____ farm animals supply us
ANOTHER TYPE OF FOOD   ADJECTIVE

with pork, _____, and bacon, and when they aren't
           PLURAL NOUN

_____, they roll around in _____.
VERB ENDING IN "ING"   TYPE OF LIQUID

MAD LIBS® is fun to play with friends, but you can also play it by yourself! To begin with, DO NOT look at the story on the page below. Fill in the blanks on this page with the words called for. Then, using the words you have selected, fill in the blank spaces in the story.

Now you've created your own hilarious MAD LIBS® game!

HOW TO STUDY

ADJECTIVE_____

ADJECTIVE_____

NOUN _____

NOUN _____

PLURAL NOUN _____

ADVERB_____

VERB _____

ADJECTIVE_____

PLURAL NOUN _____

ADJECTIVE_____

ADJECTIVE_____

ADJECTIVE_____

PLURAL NOUN _____

LETTER OF THE ALPHABET _____

MAD LIBS®
HOW TO STUDY

_____ teachers always give out _____ assignments.
　　ADJECTIVE　　　　　　　　　　　　　　　　　　ADJECTIVE

But, as everyone knows, if you want to pass all your classes so you can

go to a/an _____ and become president of a big international
　　　　　　　NOUN

_____ and have millions of _____ in the bank, you
　　NOUN　　　　　　　　　　　　　　PLURAL NOUN

must do your homework and study _____. If you just sit
　　　　　　　　　　　　　　　　　　　ADVERB

around and _____, you won't get ahead in life. You must learn
　　　　　　VERB

to pay attention to every _____ thing your teacher says. Do
　　　　　　　　　　　　ADJECTIVE

not interrupt or whisper to other _____ during class. Be
　　　　　　　　　　　　　　　PLURAL NOUN

sure to have a nice _____ notebook in which you can write
　　　　　　　　　ADJECTIVE

down anything the teacher says that seems _____. Then go
　　　　　　　　　　　　　　　　　　　ADJECTIVE

home and memorize all of these _____ notes. And when your
　　　　　　　　　　　　　　ADJECTIVE

teacher gives a surprise quiz, you will know all of the _____
　　　　　　　　　　　　　　　　　　　　　　　　　PLURAL NOUN

and will get a/an _____ as a grade for the class.
　　　　　　LETTER OF THE ALPHABET

From KID LIBS® • Copyright © 2001, 1990 by Price Stern Sloan,
a division of Penguin Putnam Books for Young Readers, New York.

MAD LIBS® is fun to play with friends, but you can also play it by yourself! To begin with, DO NOT look at the story on the page below. Fill in the blanks on this page with the words called for. Then, using the words you have selected, fill in the blank spaces in the story.

Now you've created your own hilarious MAD LIBS® game!

A TYPICAL HISTORY TEST

NOUN _____

PLURAL NOUN _____

A PLACE _____

NOUN _____

PLURAL NOUN _____

PLURAL NOUN _____

COUNTRY _____

NOUN _____

ADJECTIVE _____

PERSON IN ROOM (MALE) _____

CELEBRITY (MALE) _____

ANOTHER CELEBRITY (MALE) _____

VERB ENDING IN "ING" _____

ANOTHER CELEBRITY (MALE) _____

PLURAL NOUN _____

CELEBRITY (FEMALE) _____

MAD LIBS®
A TYPICAL HISTORY TEST

Instructions: When the _____ *rings, unfold your papers and*

NOUN

answer the following _____.

PLURAL NOUN

1. What general won the Battle of _____?

A PLACE

2. Which American _____ said, "Give me liberty or give me

NOUN

_____"?

PLURAL NOUN

3. Who was the first president of the United _____ of _____?

PLURAL NOUN   COUNTRY

4. Why did Benjamin Franklin fly a/an _____ during a

NOUN

thunderstorm?

5. Who made the first _____ flag?

ADJECTIVE

Answers to test:

1. _____

PERSON IN ROOM (MALE)

2. _____, when he was executed by _____

CELEBRITY (MALE)   ANOTHER CELEBRITY (MALE)

for _____.

VERB ENDING IN "ING"

3. _____

ANOTHER CELEBRITY (MALE)

4. He was discovering _____.

PLURAL NOUN

5. _____

CELEBRITY (FEMALE)

MAD LIBS® is fun to play with friends, but you can also play it by yourself! To begin with, DO NOT look at the story on the page below. Fill in the blanks on this page with the words called for. Then, using the words you have selected, fill in the blank spaces in the story.

Now you've created your own hilarious MAD LIBS® game!

NEW TOYS FOR KIDS

PLURAL NOUN _____

PLURAL NOUN _____

ADJECTIVE _____

PLURAL NOUN _____

PLURAL NOUN _____

NOUN _____

NAME OF PERSON (FEMALE) _____

SAME NAME _____

ARTICLE OF CLOTHING (PLURAL) _____

ADJECTIVE _____

NAME OF PERSON (MALE) _____

NOUN _____

NOUN _____

NOUN _____

SILLY WORD _____

RELATIVE _____

MAD LIBS®
NEW TOYS FOR KIDS

Commercial breaks during Saturday morning television programs are

filled with advertisements for new toys and electronic _____

PLURAL NOUN

that are supposed to educate _____. For example, there are

PLURAL NOUN

_____ versions of arcade games called "Mario and the _____"

ADJECTIVE   PLURAL NOUN

and "Mules and _____." Dolls continue to be a favorite. Today

PLURAL NOUN

you can find _____ dolls for boys, and, of course, the ever-

NOUN

popular _____ dolls for girls. Each _____ doll

NAME OF PERSON (FEMALE)   SAME NAME

needs hundreds of dollars worth of _____ and

ARTICLE OF CLOTHING (PLURAL)

has a/an _____ boyfriend named _____. And

ADJECTIVE   NAME OF PERSON (MALE)

no toy collection is complete without space toys such as the super-

powered turbo-lift _____ and the computerized robot,

NOUN

_____ which is really great because it can transform into

NOUN

a/an _____. But I guess my favorite new toy is the

NOUN

_____. I think it must be the most educational of all my

SILLY WORD

toys because even my brilliant _____ can't seem to figure out

RELATIVE

what it is or how to put it together.

From KID LIBS® • Copyright © 2001, 1990 by Price Stern Sloan,
a division of Penguin Putnam Books for Young Readers, New York.

MAD LIBS® is fun to play with friends, but you can also play it by yourself! To begin with, DO NOT look at the story on the page below. Fill in the blanks on this page with the words called for. Then, using the words you have selected, fill in the blank spaces in the story.

Now you've created your own hilarious MAD LIBS® game!

SCIENCE LAB

ADJECTIVE _____

PLURAL NOUN _____

SOMETHING ALIVE (PLURAL) _____

CELEBRITY (FEMALE) _____

PLURAL NOUN _____

PLURAL NOUN _____

PLURAL NOUN _____

ADVERB _____

ADJECTIVE _____

SOMETHING ICKY _____

NOUN _____

NOUN _____

ADJECTIVE _____

PERSON IN ROOM _____

TYPE OF CHEMICAL _____

TYPE OF FOOD _____

TYPE OF LIQUID _____

PLURAL NOUN _____

ARTICLE OF CLOTHING (PLURAL) _____

MAD LIBS®
SCIENCE LAB

Once a week, we have a science laboratory class, and we get to do

_____ experiments with _____ and _____ .
ADJECTIVE   PLURAL NOUN   SOMETHING ALIVE (PLURAL)

Our teacher, Ms. _____ , shows us how to dissect
                  CELEBRITY (FEMALE)

_____ . First, we take out the internal _____ and
PLURAL NOUN   PLURAL NOUN

_____ and draw pictures of them in our notebooks. We have
PLURAL NOUN

to work _____ or else we'll make a mess. We also learn to use
        ADVERB

chemicals to make _____ things like inexpensive household
                  ADJECTIVE

_____ and deodorizers that make a/an _____
SOMETHING ICKY   NOUN

smell like a/an _____ . Last week, we had a/an _____
                NOUN   ADJECTIVE

accident in the lab. _____ mixed some _____
                     PERSON IN ROOM   TYPE OF CHEMICAL

with _____ and added some _____ and the
     TYPE OF FOOD   TYPE OF LIQUID

mixture exploded and blew two _____ through the roof. So
                              PLURAL NOUN

now our teacher makes us all wear safety _____
                                          ARTICLE OF CLOTHING (PLURAL)

during science class.

From KID LIBS® • Copyright © 2001, 1990 by Price Stern Sloan,
a division of Penguin Putnam Books for Young Readers, New York.

MAD LIBS® is fun to play with friends, but you can also play it by yourself! To begin with, DO NOT look at the story on the page below. Fill in the blanks on this page with the words called for. Then, using the words you have selected, fill in the blank spaces in the story.

Now you've created your own hilarious MAD LIBS® game!

HOW TO GET A JOB AFTER SCHOOL

NUMBER _____

ADJECTIVE_____

PLURAL NOUN _____

TYPE OF UNPLEASANT FOOD _____

ANIMAL _____

PART OF THE BODY _____

NOUN _____

EXCLAMATION_____

NUMBER _____

TYPE OF FOOD_____

CELEBRITY _____

ANOTHER CELEBRITY _____

VERB ENDING IN "ING" _____

MAD LIBS®
HOW TO GET A JOB
AFTER SCHOOL

If you are over _____ years old, you can get a/an _____
          NUMBER   ADJECTIVE

job working for one of the _____ in the neighborhood.
                            PLURAL NOUN

Here are some tips on getting an after-school job.

1. Try not to smell like _____ or a/an _____ .
                         TYPE OF UNPLEASANT FOOD   ANIMAL

2. Have good posture. Pretend a string is tied to the top of your

_____ and keep your _____ straight.
   PART OF THE BODY   NOUN

3. Be polite. Whenever an employer asks you anything, always say,

"_____!"
  EXCLAMATION

4. Don't wear blue jeans that are more than _____ years old, and
                                             NUMBER

don't wear anything that has _____ stains on it.
                              TYPE OF FOOD

5. Work hard. Remember, the captains of industry, like _____
                                                        CELEBRITY

and _____ , all started at the bottom and became rich
    ANOTHER CELEBRITY

by _____ night and day.
   VERB ENDING IN "ING"

MAD LIBS® is fun to play with friends, but you can also play it by yourself! To begin with, DO NOT look at the story on the page below. Fill in the blanks on this page with the words called for. Then, using the words you have selected, fill in the blank spaces in the story.

Now you've created your own hilarious MAD LIBS® game!

THE ENVIRONMENT

PLURAL NOUN _____

VERB ENDING IN "ING" _____

VERB ENDING IN "ING" _____

NUMBER _____

SOMETHING ICKY _____

TYPE OF PLANT (PLURAL) _____

NOUN _____

PLURAL NOUN _____

PLURAL NOUN _____

GEOGRAPHICAL LOCATION _____

TYPE OF LIQUID _____

ADJECTIVE_____

ADJECTIVE_____

TYPE OF CONTAINER (PLURAL)_____

PLURAL NOUN _____

ADJECTIVE_____

ADJECTIVE_____

MAD LIBS®
THE ENVIRONMENT

Today, many scientists and college _____ tell us that we
                                        PLURAL NOUN

are _____ the atmosphere and _____ the
        VERB ENDING IN "ING"   VERB ENDING IN "ING"

water all over the world. In fact, in about _____ years, the air will
                                               NUMBER

be eighty percent _____ because we are cutting down
                      SOMETHING ICKY

all of the _____ in the Brazilian _____ forest.
              TYPE OF PLANT (PLURAL)   NOUN

Here in the United States, many manufacturers of toxic things like

_____ or _____ take their waste material and
   PLURAL NOUN   PLURAL NOUN

dump it into the ocean or in _____. We often have
                                GEOGRAPHICAL LOCATION

to close beaches and keep people from going into the _____
                                                        TYPE OF LIQUID

because it is so polluted. But there are some _____ things you can
                                                 ADJECTIVE

do to help protect our environment. You can write _____ letters to
                                                      ADJECTIVE

your congressperson. You can also recycle _____.
                                              TYPE OF CONTAINER (PLURAL)

With just a bit of effort, all _____ can help to make our
                                 PLURAL NOUN

planet _____ and _____ again.
          ADJECTIVE   ADJECTIVE

MAD LIBS® is fun to play with friends, but you can also play it by yourself! To begin with, DO NOT look at the story on the page below. Fill in the blanks on this page with the words called for. Then, using the words you have selected, fill in the blank spaces in the story.

Now you've created your own hilarious MAD LIBS® game!

THE GREENHOUSE EFFECT

CELEBRITY _____

ADJECTIVE _____

TYPE OF PLANT _____

ADVERB _____

TYPE OF CHEMICAL _____

ADJECTIVE _____

ADJECTIVE _____

VERB ENDING IN "ING" _____

SAME VERB ENDING IN "S" _____

STATE _____

PLACE _____

NUMBER _____

ADJECTIVE _____

PLURAL NOUN _____

PLURAL NOUN _____

VERB _____

ANOTHER PLACE _____

MAD LIBS®
THE GREENHOUSE EFFECT

_____, who is a/an _____ scientist at a very
　CELEBRITY　　　　　　　　　　ADJECTIVE

prestigious _____ League school, says that humans are
　　　　　TYPE OF PLANT

causing the earth's temperature to rise _____. This is caused
　　　　　　　　　　　　　　　　　ADVERB

by hydro-_____, which turns _____ and makes
　　　TYPE OF CHEMICAL　　　　　　ADJECTIVE

holes in the ionosphere. When the ionosphere gets _____
　　　　　　　　　　　　　　　　　　　　ADJECTIVE

enough, it starts _____. And if it _____
　　　　　VERB ENDING IN "ING"　　　　　SAME VERB ENDING IN "S"

long enough, it will melt all of the glaciers in _____ and make
　　　　　　　　　　　　　　　　　　　　STATE

the sea level rise and cover _____ to a depth of _____ feet.
　　　　　　　　　　　　PLACE　　　　　　　NUMBER

What can _____ people do about this problem? We must
　　　　　ADJECTIVE

cut down on the amount of _____ in automobile exhaust.
　　　　　　　　　　　PLURAL NOUN

We must also stop using aerosol cans because they release dangerous

_____ into the air. If this doesn't work, we'll all have to
　PLURAL NOUN

_____ to another planet. Or go to _____.
　VERB　　　　　　　　　　　　　ANOTHER PLACE

From KID LIBS® • Copyright © 2001, 1990 by Price Stern Sloan,
a division of Penguin Putnam Books for Young Readers, New York.

MAD LIBS® is fun to play with friends, but you can also play it by yourself! To begin with, DO NOT look at the story on the page below. Fill in the blanks on this page with the words called for. Then, using the words you have selected, fill in the blank spaces in the story.

Now you've created your own hilarious MAD LIBS® game!

WHAT I DID LAST SUMMER

NOUN _____

ADJECTIVE _____

ADJECTIVE _____

TYPE OF LIQUID _____

PLURAL NOUN _____

SOMETHING ALIVE (PLURAL) _____

TYPE OF FOOD (PLURAL) _____

NONSENSE WORD _____

PLURAL NOUN _____

PLURAL NOUN _____

ADJECTIVE _____

ADJECTIVE _____

VERB _____

ANOTHER TYPE OF LIQUID _____

NOUN _____

MAD LIBS®
WHAT I DID LAST SUMMER

Last summer, my father and mother took me and my older _____
                                                            NOUN

on a trip to California, which is a very _____ state with very
                                           ADJECTIVE

_____ weather. Northern California has many vineyards where
ADJECTIVE

they raise grapes to make _____ . Many old _____
                          TYPE OF LIQUID   PLURAL NOUN

go to southern California to retire and raise _____
                                              SOMETHING ALIVE (PLURAL)

or grow _____ . There are big factories in California
        TYPE OF FOOD (PLURAL)

like _____ that employ thousands of skilled
        NONSENSE WORD

_____ to make 250-seat _____ for major airlines.
PLURAL NOUN   PLURAL NOUN

Californians are politically _____ . And they are generally very
                              ADJECTIVE

_____ people who like to _____ in the sun and swim in
ADJECTIVE   VERB

_____ . And when you say goodbye to California
ANOTHER TYPE OF LIQUID

natives, they always reply, "Have a nice _____ ."
                                          NOUN

From KID LIBS® • Copyright © 2001, 1990 by Price Stern Sloan,
a division of Penguin Putnam Books for Young Readers, New York.

MAD LIBS® is fun to play with friends, but you can also play it by yourself! To begin with, DO NOT look at the story on the page below. Fill in the blanks on this page with the words called for. Then, using the words you have selected, fill in the blank spaces in the story.

Now you've created your own hilarious MAD LIBS® game!

WHAT NOT TO EAT
FOR LUNCH

ADVERB _____

TYPE OF CONTAINER _____

ADJECTIVE _____

ADJECTIVE _____

SOMETHING ICKY _____

ANIMAL _____

NOUN _____

SILLY WORD _____

PLURAL NOUN _____

VERB ENDING IN "ING" _____

ADJECTIVE _____

ANOTHER SILLY WORD _____

TYPE OF FOOD _____

PLURAL NOUN _____

ANOTHER ANIMAL _____

COUNTRY _____

MAD LIBS®
WHAT NOT TO EAT
FOR LUNCH

Everyone knows that kids who eat junk food turn out _____ .
ADVERB

Make sure your lunch _____ is filled with nutritious
TYPE OF CONTAINER

_____ food. Do not go to the _____ food stand across
ADJECTIVE ADJECTIVE

the street from your school. The hamburgers they serve are fried in

_____ and are made of _____ meat. The hotdogs con-
SOMETHING ICKY ANIMAL

tain chemicals such as hydrogenated _____ and sodium
NOUN

_____ . And they are made from ground-up _____ .
SILLY WORD PLURAL NOUN

If you spend time _____ around those places,
VERB ENDING IN "ING"

you will get fat and _____ and people will call you a/an
ADJECTIVE

_____ . So take a sandwich made of chicken or turkey
ANOTHER SILLY WORD

and lettuce or _____ and _____ . And drink healthy
TYPE OF FOOD PLURAL NOUN

_____ milk instead of chemical cola drinks. If you eat
ANOTHER ANIMAL

good food, you might grow up to become president of _____ .
COUNTRY

From KID LIBS® • Copyright © 2001, 1990 by Price Stern Sloan,
a division of Penguin Putnam Books for Young Readers, New York.

MAD LIBS® is fun to play with friends, but you can also play it by yourself! To begin with, DO NOT look at the story on the page below. Fill in the blanks on this page with the words called for. Then, using the words you have selected, fill in the blank spaces in the story.

Now you've created your own hilarious MAD LIBS® game!

BREAKFAST

PIECE OF FURNITURE _____

TYPE OF FOOD _____

FIVE LETTERS OF THE ALPHABET _____

ADJECTIVE _____

ADJECTIVE _____

ANOTHER TYPE OF FOOD _____

PLURAL NOUN _____

SILLY WORD _____

LAST NAME OF PERSON _____

TYPE OF VEGETABLE _____

TYPE OF LIQUID _____

NUMBER _____

NUMBER _____

SOMETHING GREASY _____

ANOTHER TYPE OF LIQUID _____

ANOTHER TYPE OF FOOD _____

MAD LIBS
BREAKFAST

Supermarkets devote 30% of their _____ space
PIECE OF FURNITURE

to breakfast cereal. The cereals all contain niacin, more fiber than a

pound of _____, and vitamins _____ .
TYPE OF FOOD   FIVE LETTERS OF THE ALPHABET

Every kid should start off his or her day with a healthy breakfast to

get energy for another _____ day at his or her _____
ADJECTIVE   ADJECTIVE

school. First, you have a glass of _____ juice. Then the
ANOTHER TYPE OF FOOD

cereal. You have a choice of Fortified Oat _____ or Sugar-
PLURAL NOUN

Coated _____ or Captain _____ or _____
SILLY WORD   LAST NAME OF PERSON   TYPE OF VEGETABLE

Crispies. Eat this with sugar and homogenized _____ .
TYPE OF LIQUID

Follow this with _____ eggs and _____ slices of bacon
NUMBER   NUMBER

and toast spread with melted _____ . Then have a
SOMETHING GREASY

cup of delicious hot _____ with a spoonful of
ANOTHER TYPE OF LIQUID

_____ in it. And you are ready to go off to school.
ANOTHER TYPE OF FOOD

From KID LIBS® • Copyright © 2001, 1990 by Price Stern Sloan,
a division of Penguin Putnam Books for Young Readers, New York.

MAD LIBS® is fun to play with friends, but you can also play it by yourself! To begin with, DO NOT look at the story on the page below. Fill in the blanks on this page with the words called for. Then, using the words you have selected, fill in the blank spaces in the story.

Now you've created your own hilarious MAD LIBS® game!

NOTES TO TEACHER

NAME OF TEACHER _____

PERSON IN ROOM (MALE)_____

PART OF THE BODY _____

NOUN _____

ADJECTIVE_____

NUMBER _____

NUMBER _____

NUMBER _____

VERB _____

PLURAL NOUN _____

ADJECTIVE_____

PLURAL NOUN _____

PLURAL NOUN _____

COLOR_____

PLURAL NOUN _____

NOUN _____

MAD LIBS®
NOTES TO TEACHER

Dear _____,
          NAME OF TEACHER

I am writing to ask you to excuse my son, _____,
                                              PERSON IN ROOM (MALE)

from math class. Trying to do his homework has given him a pain in

the _____. This has caused him to be unable to use a/an
        PART OF THE BODY

_____. He is just like his _____ father, who adds
        NOUN   ADJECTIVE

_____ and _____ and always comes up with _____.
  NUMBER   NUMBER   NUMBER

If you excuse him, he will stay after school and _____ the
                                                        VERB

blackboards and dust the _____.
                            PLURAL NOUN

Dear Principal,

Please forgive my daughter for missing her _____ classes
                                                ADJECTIVE

yesterday. I had to take her to the dentist to get her _____
                                                          PLURAL NOUN

cleaned and have her _____ measured for braces so that
                        PLURAL NOUN

when she is older, she will have straight _____ _____.
                                            COLOR   PLURAL NOUN

If you excuse her, I will send you a homemade _____.

From KID LIBS® • Copyright © 2001, 1990 by Price Stern Sloan,
a division of Penguin Putnam Books for Young Readers, New York.

MAD LIBS® is fun to play with friends, but you can also play it by yourself! To begin with, DO NOT look at the story on the page below. Fill in the blanks on this page with the words called for. Then, using the words you have selected, fill in the blank spaces in the story.

Now you've created your own hilarious MAD LIBS® game!

GEOGRAPHY PART I

ADJECTIVE _____

ADJECTIVE _____

PLURAL NOUN _____

ADJECTIVE _____

PLURAL NOUN _____

PLURAL NOUN _____

PLURAL NOUN _____

PLURAL NOUN _____

PLURAL NOUN _____

VERB ENDING IN "ING" _____

FOREIGN CITY _____

A PLACE _____

ADJECTIVE _____

CITY _____

ADVERB _____

ADVERB _____

MAD LIBS®
GEOGRAPHY PART I

_____ experts have taken many _____ polls that
   ADJECTIVE   ADJECTIVE

indicate that most American _____ who attend the average
                               PLURAL NOUN

American _____ school don't know anything about geography.
         ADJECTIVE

These _____ don't know much about _____ or
     PLURAL NOUN   PLURAL NOUN

_____ either, but geography is important because it teaches
  PLURAL NOUN

us where all the continents, countries, states, and _____ are.
                                      PLURAL NOUN

Geography also helps us learn the capitals of all the _____
                                          PLURAL NOUN

and is just as important as math or English or _____.
                                   VERB ENDING IN "ING"

Besides, if you don't know anything about geography, you might start

traveling to _____ from Fort Worth, Texas, and end up in
           FOREIGN CITY

_____. Or maybe you'd end up in a really _____ town
 A PLACE   ADJECTIVE

like _____. So the next time you have geography class, listen
    CITY

_____ to your teacher and study _____.
  ADVERB   ADVERB

MAD LIBS® is fun to play with friends, but you can also play it by yourself! To begin with, DO NOT look at the story on the page below. Fill in the blanks on this page with the words called for. Then, using the words you have selected, fill in the blank spaces in the story.

Now you've created your own hilarious MAD LIBS® game!

GEOGRAPHY PART II

ADJECTIVE_____

TYPE OF LIQUID _____

SILLY WORD_____

PLURAL NOUN _____

ADJECTIVE_____

A PLACE _____

FOREIGN COUNTRY _____

TOWN_____

STATE_____

NOUN _____

ANOTHER PLACE _____

NUMBER _____

ANOTHER FOREIGN COUNTRY _____

ANOTHER STATE_____

ANOTHER STATE_____

PERSON IN ROOM _____

MAD LIBS®
GEOGRAPHY PART II

Here are some _____ geographical facts that you should know.
ADJECTIVE

1. A peninsula is an area of land surrounded by _____ and
TYPE OF LIQUID

connected to the mainland by a/an _____ .
SILLY WORD

2. Texas has more _____ and more _____ cows
PLURAL NOUN   ADJECTIVE

than _____ .
A PLACE

3. The capital of _____ is _____ .
FOREIGN COUNTRY   TOWN

4. The Grand Canyon in _____ is the largest _____
STATE   NOUN

in the world.

5. The Mississippi River runs from _____ through _____
ANOTHER PLACE   NUMBER

states and winds up in the Gulf of _____ .
ANOTHER FOREIGN COUNTRY

6. Montana is bordered by _____ on the north, by
ANOTHER STATE

_____ on the west, and by _____ on the south.
ANOTHER STATE   PERSON IN ROOM

From KID LIBS® • Copyright © 2001, 1990 by Price Stern Sloan,
a division of Penguin Putnam Books for Young Readers, New York.

MAD LIBS® is fun to play with friends, but you can also play it by yourself! To begin with, DO NOT look at the story on the page below. Fill in the blanks on this page with the words called for. Then, using the words you have selected, fill in the blank spaces in the story.

Now you've created your own hilarious MAD LIBS® game!

WHAT TO DO AT RECESS

COLOR_____

VERB ENDING IN "ING" _____

PART OF THE BODY _____

ANIMAL _____

VERB ENDING IN "ING" _____

TYPE OF FOOD _____

ROOM _____

PERSON IN ROOM _____

VERB ENDING IN "ING" _____

ANOTHER ROOM _____

NOUN _____

PLURAL NOUN _____

PLURAL NOUN _____

ADJECTIVE_____

NOUN _____

MAD LIBS®
WHAT TO DO AT RECESS

Any _____ -blooded American kid likes recess better
<u>COLOR</u>

than _____ in a classroom. Here are some things to
<u>VERB ENDING IN "ING"</u>

do at recess.

1. Start a game of "touch" _____-ball.
<u>PART OF THE BODY</u>

2. Put a/an _____ in someone's lunch box.
<u>ANIMAL</u>

3. Challenge the school bully to a _____ contest.
<u>VERB ENDING IN "ING"</u>

4. Start a/an _____ fight in the school _____ .
<u>TYPE OF FOOD</u>   <u>ROOM</u>

5. Report _____ to the principal for _____
<u>PERSON IN ROOM</u>   <u>VERB ENDING IN "ING"</u>

   in the _____ .
<u>ANOTHER ROOM</u>

6. Choose up sides and have a _____-painting tournament.
<u>NOUN</u>

7. Start a strike against the school demanding more _____
<u>PLURAL NOUN</u>

   and shorter _____ .
<u>PLURAL NOUN</u>

8. Collect money from all of the students and buy your favorite

   _____ teacher a new _____ .
<u>ADJECTIVE</u>   <u>NOUN</u>

MAD LIBS® is fun to play with friends, but you can also play it by yourself! To begin with, DO NOT look at the story on the page below. Fill in the blanks on this page with the words called for. Then, using the words you have selected, fill in the blank spaces in the story.

Now you've created your own hilarious MAD LIBS® game!

PHYSICAL EDUCATION CLASS

ADJECTIVE _____

TYPE OF GAME _____

TYPE OF CONTAINER _____

PLURAL NOUN _____

ADJECTIVE _____

PLURAL NOUN _____

PLURAL NOUN _____

PART OF THE BODY _____

ADJECTIVE _____

NUMBER _____

NOUN _____

SOMETHING ROUND _____

SOMETHING HEAVY (PLURAL) _____

NUMBER _____

PLURAL NOUN _____

A PLACE _____

TYPE OF LIQUID _____

VERB ENDING IN "ING" _____

MAD LIBS®
PHYSICAL EDUCATION CLASS

All _____ schools have physical education classes. The teacher
         ADJECTIVE

is usually the _____ coach and everyone gets a metal
              TYPE OF GAME

_____ in which to put their _____ when they put
TYPE OF CONTAINER   PLURAL NOUN

on their gym suits. First, the phys. ed. teacher makes all the students

do _____ exercises to warm up their _____. He
       ADJECTIVE   PLURAL NOUN

or she will say, "_____ on hips. Now everyone do a full
                     PLURAL NOUN

_____ bend!" You will have to hold this _____
PART OF THE BODY   ADJECTIVE

position until your gym teacher counts up to _____ or until
                                              NUMBER

one of the students in the _____ faints. Then your teacher
                            NOUN

will make everyone play volley _____ or lift heavy
                                SOMETHING ROUND

_____. After what seems like _____ hours,
SOMETHING HEAVY (PLURAL)   NUMBER

your teacher will make all of the _____ run around
                                   PLURAL NOUN

_____ until they are dripping with _____ and
A PLACE   TYPE OF LIQUID

panting and _____.
             VERB ENDING IN "ING"

From KID LIBS® • Copyright © 2001, 1990 by Price Stern Sloan,
a division of Penguin Putnam Books for Young Readers, New York.

MAD LIBS® is fun to play with friends, but you can also play it by yourself! To begin with, DO NOT look at the story on the page below. Fill in the blanks on this page with the words called for. Then, using the words you have selected, fill in the blank spaces in the story.

Now you've created your own hilarious MAD LIBS® game!

MY FAVORITE TEACHER CONTEST

ADJECTIVE _____

CELEBRITY (FEMALE) _____

ADJECTIVE _____

SCHOOL _____

PLURAL NOUN _____

ADJECTIVE _____

ADJECTIVE _____

PART OF THE BODY _____

CELEBRITY (MALE) _____

ADJECTIVE _____

NOUN _____

VERB _____

CELEBRITY _____

LETTER OF THE ALPHABET _____

ROOM _____

PLURAL NOUN _____

PIECE OF FURNITURE _____

NOUN _____

MAD☺LIBS®
MY FAVORITE TEACHER
CONTEST

Dear School Board,

I heard you were running a contest to pick the most _____
                                                      ADJECTIVE

teacher in town. I would like to nominate _____ , who
                                           CELEBRITY (FEMALE)

teaches history and _____ studies at _____ . She is
                     ADJECTIVE   SCHOOL

always patient with her _____ , no matter how _____
                         PLURAL NOUN   ADJECTIVE

or _____ we get. Yesterday she asked, "Who is president
   ADJECTIVE

of the United States?" and I held up my _____ and said,
                                          PART OF THE BODY

" _____ ." My answer was incorrect, but she didn't get
   CELEBRITY (MALE)

_____ or hit me with a _____ or even make me
 ADJECTIVE   NOUN

_____ in the corner. She gave me a second chance and asked,
 VERB

"Who is buried in Grant's Tomb?" I knew that one. I answered,

" _____ ." And for a grade, she gave me _____ .
   CELEBRITY   LETTER OF THE ALPHABET

She also doesn't mind when we have to go to the _____
                                                     ROOM

and doesn't get mad if we throw _____ or hide under the
                                  PLURAL NOUN

_____ . I hope you pick her as the world's best _____ .
 PIECE OF FURNITURE   NOUN

From KID LIBS® • Copyright © 2001, 1990 by Price Stern Sloan,
a division of Penguin Putnam Books for Young Readers, New York.

MAD LIBS® is fun to play with friends, but you can also play it by yourself! To begin with, DO NOT look at the story on the page below. Fill in the blanks on this page with the words called for. Then, using the words you have selected, fill in the blank spaces in the story.

Now you've created your own hilarious MAD LIBS® game!

SCENE BETWEEN A PARENT AND A TEACHER

PERSON IN ROOM _____

ANOTHER PERSON IN ROOM _____

SCHOOL _____

PERSON IN ROOM (MALE)_____

NOUN _____

PLURAL NOUN _____

NOUN _____

NOUN _____

ADJECTIVE_____

PLURAL NOUN _____

PERSON IN ROOM (FEMALE)_____

ARTICLE OF CLOTHING_____

ADVERB_____

NOUN _____

ADJECTIVE_____

MAD LIBS®
SCENE BETWEEN A PARENT
AND A TEACHER

(To be read by _____ *and* _____*.)*
                      PERSON IN ROOM   ANOTHER PERSON IN ROOM

TEACHER: I asked you to come to _____ because I am so
                                          SCHOOL

worried about your son, _____ .
                               PERSON IN ROOM (MALE)

PARENT: Oh, I am sure he has been a very good _____ .
                                                        NOUN

We have always taught him to mind his _____ .
                                              PLURAL NOUN

TEACHER: Well, yesterday I caught him copying from someone

else's _____ .
             NOUN

PARENT: I cannot believe that our little _____ would do
                                                   NOUN

anything that _____ .
                    ADJECTIVE

TEACHER: And on Monday, he stole three _____ from
                                                 PLURAL NOUN

_____ 's _____ .
PERSON IN ROOM (FEMALE)   ARTICLE OF CLOTHING

PARENT: Well, he always behaves very _____ at home.
                                               ADVERB

TEACHER;   I hope you will talk to your _____ about these
                                                NOUN

problems.

PARENT: I will, I will. I'll ground him and take away his _____
                                                                   ADJECTIVE

privileges.

MAD LIBS® is fun to play with friends, but you can also play it by yourself! To begin with, DO NOT look at the story on the page below. Fill in the blanks on this page with the words called for. Then, using the words you have selected, fill in the blank spaces in the story.

Now you've created your own hilarious MAD LIBS® game!

FUTURE TECHNOLOGY IN AMERICA

TYPE OF APPLIANCE _____

NUMBER _____

ADJECTIVE _____

TYPE OF INVENTION _____

ANOTHER TYPE OF INVENTION _____

ADVERB _____

PLURAL NOUN _____

A PLACE _____

ADJECTIVE _____

VERB ENDING IN "ING" _____

PLURAL NOUN _____

NOUN _____

PLURAL NOUN _____

PLURAL NOUN _____

PLURAL NOUN _____

PLURAL NOUN _____

VERB ENDING IN "ING" _____

VERB ENDING IN "ING" _____

MAD LIBS®
FUTURE TECHNOLOGY
IN AMERICA

Can you imagine having to live without a/an _____ ?
TYPE OF APPLIANCE

Well, just _____ years ago, most Americans lived a very _____
NUMBER ADJECTIVE

life. But then, with the introduction of _____ and
TYPE OF INVENTION

_____ , daily life changed _____ .
ANOTHER TYPE OF INVENTION ADVERB

Some _____ think that living in _____ has
PLURAL NOUN A PLACE

become too complicated. But just think about what the _____
ADJECTIVE

future will bring. Instead of _____ our cars on the free-
VERB ENDING IN "ING"

way, we'll be able to fly in small _____ . If you are very lucky,
PLURAL NOUN

you might own a supersonic _____ . And you'll probably own
NOUN

at least one or two digital _____ and a few super-automated
PLURAL NOUN

photon _____ . Of course, we'll all have robots who will
PLURAL NOUN

cook our _____ and clean our _____ . In fact,
PLURAL NOUN PLURAL NOUN

some day, machines will do everything for us, and we'll spend every

day just _____ and _____ .
VERB ENDING IN "ING" VERB ENDING IN "ING"